I Declare War

Spiritual Warfare

Sherrell Attaway

*Equipping believers to fight, stand, and win
through the Word of God*

Dedication

I dedicate this book…
First and foremost, to God
For keeping me, covering me, and calling me…
even when I didn't understand it.
For never giving up on me,
even when I gave up on myself.
For turning my pain into purpose
and my brokenness into a testimony.

To my husband, Damien Attaway
My life partner, my business partner, and my soulmate.
Thank you for standing with me, believing in me,
and walking this journey with me.
May God continue to use both of us
to reach the multitude for His glory.

To my beautiful daughters
Damieona, Damiela, and Destiny
You are my heartbeats.
My prayer is that God gives you wisdom to build,
strength to stand, and faith to trust Him in every season.
May your lives be rooted and grounded in God's Word,
and may you always know your worth.

To my grandchildren
Kyree Seymour, Khorey Seymour, and Charmani Smith
May God open doors that no man can shut.
May your lives be built on truth, faith, and purpose.

To my parents
In loving memory of my father, Jerry Robinson

thank you for teaching me to keep trusting, keep believing, and to
work hard.
Your legacy lives on through me.
To my mother, Dorthy Edwards
thank you for carrying me, covering me in prayer,
and loving me through every season of my life.

To my last living biological uncle, Lloyd Taylor
(my father's brother)
You have been the glue that holds our family together.
You have always been there when I needed you.
Your strength, your presence, and your love
have meant more than words can express.

To my biological aunt, Gloria Reid
(my father's sister)
Thank you for your presence in my life
and for the legacy we share through family.

To My Prayer Partners
Thank you for keeping me accountable,
for covering me in prayer,
and for standing in the gap for me when I needed it most.
Your prayers strengthened me.
Your consistency encouraged me.
Your faith helped carry me through seasons
I could not have survived alone.
You are a vital part of this journey…
and I am forever grateful.

To every person who has ever felt broken, overlooked, or unworthy
This book is for you.
May you find healing in these pages.
May you discover your worth.
And may you walk boldly in your purpose.

Final Note
This is more than a book…
This is a piece of my life.
And I pray it changes yours.

Table of Contents

Introduction

A Call to War

This is not motivation.
This is not inspiration.

This is activation.

You are not just dealing with life…
You are in a spiritual war.

And whether you realize it or not

You've been fighting.

Now you will learn how to win

Chapter 1:
You Are in A War

Many people believe life is just a series of events
good days, bad days, ups and downs.

They go through life reacting to what they see,
adjusting to circumstances,
and trying to manage whatever comes their way.

But as a believer, you must understand:

What you see in the natural
is often being influenced by something spiritual.

There is always more happening than what meets the eye.

Everything happens in the spiritual
before it manifests in the natural.

Which means what you are seeing
did not start where you think it did.

It may look like it started with a conversation…
a situation…
a delay…
or even a decision.

But the root of it
the origin of it
is deeper than that.

You Are Not Just Dealing With What You See

You are not just dealing with:

Stress
People

Delays
Emotions

Those are only the surface.

There is a deeper reality.

There is an unseen realm that influences what is seen.

There is a battle that is not always visible
but it is always active.

There is an enemy.

Understand Your Enemy

You must also understand this clearly:

The enemy hates you.

Not sometimes.
Not occasionally.

Always.

He is not neutral toward you.
He is not undecided about you.

He is not your friend.

Even when he comes appearing friendly…
even when it looks harmless…
even when it feels comfortable…

He is not for you.

He comes with a strategy.

He comes with intention.

He comes with:

Deception

Distraction
Division

His goal is never to help you
it is to hinder you.

To slow you down.
To confuse you.
To pull you off course.

The Moment Everything Changed

The moment you gave your life to God,
you stepped into a different reality.

You didn't just make a decision
you entered a spiritual dimension.

A reality where:

Light and darkness oppose each other

Truth is constantly challenged by deception

Purpose is attacked by distraction

There is no neutral ground here.

You are either advancing…
or you are being resisted.

Scripture

Ephesians 6:12
"For we wrestle not against flesh and blood, but against principalities…"

This Means Something Specific

This means:

Your battle is not really with people.

Even when it feels personal.
Even when it looks intentional.
Even when it hurts.

It may look like:

Conflict with others

Frustration in relationships

Opposition at work

Pressure in your mind

But behind it…

There is something spiritual at work.

The Wrong Fight

One of the greatest strategies of the enemy
is to keep you focused on the wrong fight.

If he can keep you:

Blaming people

Fighting in your flesh

Reacting emotionally

Then you will never address the real source.

And if you never address the real source…
you will keep repeating the same battles.

Different people.

Same frustration.

Different situations.
Same outcome.

Because the root was never confronted.

Why You Feel Exhausted

Many believers are exhausted
not because the battle is too hard…

But because they are fighting the wrong way.

They are trying to solve spiritual problems
with natural effort.

You don't win this war by:

Arguing harder

Worrying more

Trying to control everything

Overthinking every situation

That only drains you.

That only frustrates you.

That only keeps you stuck in cycles.

How You Actually Win

You win by:

Discernment

The Word of God

Spiritual authority

You win when you stop reacting
and start discerning.

You win when you stop guessing
and start knowing.

You win when you stop fighting people
and start addressing the spirit behind it.

Key Insight

What you don't discern,
you will mismanage.

And what you mismanage
will continue to repeat.

Let that settle.

Because this is where many people stay stuck.

Not because they don't pray.
Not because they don't believe.

But because they don't **discern correctly**.

The Enemy Studies You

The enemy studies patterns.

He watches:

What triggers you

What frustrates you

What distracts you

Where you are inconsistent

If he finds what triggers you,
he will keep using it.

If he finds where you are weak,
he will keep pressing it.

If he finds where you lack knowledge,
he will build strongholds there.

He is not random.

He is strategic.

But Today It Breaks

But today that cycle breaks.

Not because something changed around you…

But because something is changing **within you**.

You are becoming aware.

You are becoming discerning.

You are no longer blind to what has been operating.

Declaration

Say this out loud:

"I will no longer fight the wrong battles.
God is opening my eyes to see clearly.

I understand that everything begins in the spirit,
and I will not be deceived by appearances.

I discern truth from deception.
I am equipped, aware, and aligned with God's Word."

Prayer

Father God,

Thank You for opening my understanding.

Help me to see beyond what is in front of me.
Give me discernment to recognize what is spiritual
and not just natural.

Expose every form of deception in my life.
Teach me to recognize the enemy's tactics clearly.

Break every cycle in my life
that has been fueled by misunderstanding.

From this day forward,
I choose to fight with clarity,
authority, and truth.

In Jesus' name,
Amen.

Chapter 2:
The Battlefield Of The Mind

One of the greatest battles you will ever face
will not be around you…

It will be within you.

Not in your environment.
Not in your relationships.
Not even in your circumstances.

But in your mind.

Because long before anything shows up in your life
it has already passed through your thoughts.

The Real Battlefield

The mind is the primary battlefield
where spiritual warfare takes place.

This is where decisions are formed.
This is where beliefs are established.
This is where truth is either accepted… or rejected.

Before the enemy attacks your life,
he targets your thoughts.

He doesn't start with your finances.
He doesn't start with your relationships.

He starts with your thinking.

Because if he can control your thoughts,
he can influence your actions.

And if he can influence your actions,

he can shape your life.

The Process

Everything begins in the spirit…
but it is processed through your mind.

Which means:

What you think about matters.

What you allow to stay matters.

What you entertain matters.

Because your mind becomes the filter
through which everything flows.

A Powerful Tool—or a Dangerous Place

The mind is a powerful tool.

But it can also become a dangerous place
when left unguarded.

An unguarded mind
is an open door.

And the enemy will always walk through
an open door.

The Mind Will Betray You If You Let It

The mind will play tricks on you.

It will make you believe things
that are not true.

It will:

Magnify fear

Replay pain

Distort reality

Make temporary situations feel permanent

Make small issues feel overwhelming

If you don't recognize what's happening,
you will start agreeing with it.

The Enemy's Strategy

The enemy understands this:

If he can plant a thought,
and you believe it…

it becomes your reality.

He doesn't need control of your life.
He only needs influence over your thinking.

Because once you agree with a lie
you will live it out as truth.

The Whispers

He whispers things like:

"You're not good enough"

"This will never work"

"God has forgotten about you"

"You will always be like this"

"You'll never change"

"You're too far gone"

And if you don't recognize it…

you will receive it.

And once you receive it…
you will start responding to it.

Scripture

2 Corinthians 10:5
"Casting down imaginations, and every high thing that exalteth itself against the knowledge of God…"

What This Means

This reveals something powerful:

Not every thought comes from you.

Every thought you think
did not originate with you.

Some thoughts are:

Planted

Suggested

Strategically sent

The enemy does not need to force you
he only needs to influence you.

The Danger of Agreement

A thought only has power
when it goes unchallenged.

If you let it sit
it grows.

If you entertain it

it strengthens.

If you agree with it
it becomes part of you.

Why Many Believers Struggle

Many believers struggle
not because they lack faith…

But because they entertain the wrong thoughts.

They pray…
but think negatively.

They believe God…
but expect failure.

They speak faith…
but meditate on fear.

And you cannot live in victory
while constantly thinking in defeat.

You Have More Control Than You Think

You cannot stop a thought from coming…

But you can stop it from staying.

You have authority over what you allow.

You have authority over what you repeat.

You have authority over what you agree with.

Key Insight

If you don't take control of your thoughts,
your thoughts will take control of you.

There is no middle ground.

You are either governing your mind
or your mind is governing you.

What Happens in the Mind

The battlefield of your mind is where:

Fear tries to grow

Doubt tries to settle

Lies try to become truth

Confusion tries to take over

Insecurity tries to define you

But God has given you authority even here.

Your Authority

You have the power to:

Reject lies

Replace thoughts

Align your mind with God's Word

You are not a victim of your thoughts.

You are the authority over them.

Scripture Alignment

Philippians 2:5
"Let this mind be in you, which was also in Christ Jesus."

What This Requires

This means you are not called
to think like the world…

You are called to think like Christ.

That requires:

Intentional thinking

Discipline

Awareness

Alignment with truth

Your Strategy

You don't fight thoughts with emotions.

You fight thoughts with truth.

When the enemy says:
"You're not enough"

You respond with the Word.

When the enemy says:
"You will fail"

You respond with the Word.

When the enemy says:
"Nothing is changing"

You respond with the Word.

Because truth cancels lies.

Scripture Reinforcement

Romans 12:2
"Be transformed by the renewing of your mind…"

Renewal Is Necessary

Renewing your mind is not optional.

It is required for transformation.

If your mind is not renewed
your life will not change.

You cannot think the same
and expect different results.

Daily Discipline

Renewing your mind is not a one-time event.

It is daily.

It is consistent.

It is intentional.

You must:

Watch what you listen to

Watch what you entertain

Watch what you repeat

Because what you repeatedly hear
will shape what you believe.

Power Principle

What you repeatedly think
will eventually shape how you live.

Your life will always move
in the direction of your dominant thoughts.

So the question is:

Who is influencing your thoughts?

God…
or the enemy?

Truth…
or deception?

Declaration

Say this out loud:

"I take authority over my mind.

Every thought that is not from God
is rejected.

I cast down every lie, every fear,
and every negative imagination.

My mind is renewed by the Word of God.
I think like Christ,
and I walk in truth and victory."

Prayer

Father God,

Thank You for giving me authority
even over my thoughts.

Help me to recognize every lie
that tries to enter my mind.

Give me the discipline to reject what is not from You
and the wisdom to replace it with truth.

Renew my mind daily through Your Word.
Let the mind of Christ be in me.

Remove every pattern of thinking
that does not align with Your will.

From this day forward,
my mind is guarded,
my thoughts are aligned,
and my life reflects Your truth.

In Jesus' name,

Chapter 3:
Your Weapon The Word Of God

Many believers know the Word…

They've heard it.
They've read it.
They can even quote it.

But they don't use the Word.

And that is where the disconnect happens.

Because there is a difference between:

Reading the Word

Quoting the Word

And fighting with the Word

And until you move from reading…
to using…

You will continue to have access to power
without ever releasing it.

The Word Is Not Just Information

The Word of God is not just information.

It is not just something to encourage you.
It is not just something to study.

It is a weapon.

Scripture

Hebrews 4:12
"For the word of God is quick, and powerful, and sharper than any two-edged sword…"

What This Really Means

This means the Word is:

Alive
Powerful
Active

It is not passive.

It is not inactive.

It is not waiting.

It is moving.

It is working.

It is responding when it is released.

What the Word Does

The Word cuts through:

Lies

Fear

Deception

Strongholds

Confusion

Doubt

It doesn't negotiate with the problem.

It **cuts through it**.

The Enemy Knows This

The enemy is not afraid of a Bible on your shelf.

He is not intimidated by what you own.

He is not moved by what you highlight.

He is afraid of the Word in your mouth.

Because once the Word is spoken in faith…

It becomes active.

Silence Is Not Neutral

Truth:

A silent believer
is an unarmed believer.

You cannot stay quiet
and expect victory.

The power of the Word
is released when it is spoken.

Not just read.
Not just thought about.

Spoken.

Jesus Showed Us How to Fight

When Jesus was tempted,
He did not argue…

He did not panic…

He did not negotiate…

He did not explain Himself…

He responded with:

"It is written."

Scripture Example

Matthew 4:4
"It is written, Man shall not live by bread alone…"

Every Attack Was Answered the Same Way

Every time the enemy came…

Jesus didn't change strategies.

He didn't try something new.

He didn't rely on emotion.

He responded with the Word.

Every. Single. Time.

Key Insight

If Jesus used the Word to fight
why wouldn't you?

You are not called to create your own strategy.

You are called to use what already works.

Why Many Believers Lose

Many believers lose battles
not because they don't love God…

But because they don't respond with the Word.

They respond with:

Feelings

Fear

Frustration

Silence

Overthinking

Complaining

And none of those defeat the enemy.

Feelings don't defeat the enemy.

Logic doesn't defeat the enemy.

Effort doesn't defeat the enemy.

The Word does.

This Is Where Power Happens

Application is where power is released.

Knowing the Word is important…

But knowing when to apply the Word
to your situation is powerful.

Because timing matters.

Awareness matters.

Discernment matters.

What You Must Do

When you are facing something:

Grab a scripture from the Bible
and stand on it.

Not casually.

Not temporarily.

Stand on it.

Hold it close to your heart.
Speak it.
Believe it.
Repeat it.

Even when you don't feel it.

Especially when you don't feel it.

You Don't Need to Know Everything

You don't have to know the whole Bible.

You don't have to be a Bible scholar.

You don't have to have every scripture memorized.

But you do have to be a believer
who knows how to use what you know.

Scripture Reminder

1 Corinthians 10:13
"There hath no temptation taken you but such as is common to man…"

What This Means

What you are facing is not new.

It may feel personal…
but it is not unique.

And God has already provided
a way through it.

That means:

You are not stuck.
You are not trapped.
You are not outmatched.

Let the Word Do the Work

Truth:

Let His Word do the work.

You don't have to force results.
You don't have to fight in your own strength.
You don't have to figure everything out.

You stand on the Word…

And the Word fights for you.

Your Strategy Moving Forward

You must learn to:

Speak the Word

Declare the Word

Stand on the Word

Not occasionally.
Not when it's convenient.

Consistently.

How You Respond Matters

When fear shows up,
you don't entertain it you confront it.

When doubt speaks,
you don't agree you override it.

When confusion rises,
you don't sit in it you address it.

With what?

The Word.

Power Principle

What you speak consistently
you will begin to see manifested.

Your words are not empty.

Your words are not casual.

Your words carry weight.

Scripture Reinforcement

Proverbs 18:21
"Death and life are in the power of the tongue…"

Your Mouth Is a Weapon

This means your mouth
is not just for talking…

It is for warfare.

What you say:

Matters

Builds

Destroys

Aligns

Activates

Reality Check

If you don't speak the Word,
you leave room for the enemy to speak louder.

Silence creates space.

And the enemy will always fill empty space.

Activation

Stop waiting for change
and start declaring truth.

You don't say:
"I'm overwhelmed"

You say:
"God is my peace"

You don't say:
"I'm stuck"

You say:
"God is making a way"

You don't say:
"This isn't working"

You say:

"All things are working together for my good"

Because the Word shifts the atmosphere.

Declaration

Say this out loud:

"The Word of God is my weapon.

I know how to apply the Word to my life.
I stand on His promises and hold them in my heart.

Every lie is broken by the truth of God's Word.
Every attack is answered with 'It is written.'

I am equipped, empowered,
and dangerous to the enemy."

Prayer

Father God,

Thank You for giving me Your Word
as a weapon.

Teach me not just to read it,
but to apply it.

Show me what to stand on
in every season of my life.

Give me boldness to speak truth
even when I don't feel it.

Let Your Word live in me,
rest in my heart,
and come out of my mouth with power.

From this day forward,
I will trust Your Word

and let it do the work.

In Jesus' name,
Amen.

Chapter 4:
Breaking Strongholds

Many believers love God…

They pray.
They believe.
They show up.

But they still struggle with the same patterns.

The same thoughts.
The same habits.
The same cycles.

Over and over again.

What they thought would be temporary…
has become repetitive.

What they thought they were free from…
keeps showing back up.

This is not random.

This is a stronghold.

What a Stronghold Really Is

A stronghold is not just a behavior.

It is deeper than actions.

It is a way of thinking
that has been reinforced over time
until it feels normal.

It becomes familiar.

It becomes automatic.

It becomes something you stop questioning.

And that is what makes it dangerous.

Because when something feels normal…
you stop fighting it.

My Reality

I dealt with so many demons in my past…

Being molested.
Dealing with domestic situations.
Using drugs.
Partying.
Drinking.

The death of my father…

While married, facing divorce…

If you name it…
it found me.

And for a long time,
it didn't just touch my life…

It shaped my thinking.

Deliverance Is Not Just External

Even after I was physically delivered…
I was still mentally bound.

I was out of the situation…
but the situation was still in me.

Because deliverance is not just physical.

It is mental.
It is spiritual.
It is internal.

You can leave something…
and still carry it.

You can walk away…
and still think like it.

The Turning Point

And it wasn't until
the love of the Lord Jesus Christ
wrapped me in His arms and fathered me…

That I began to truly heal.

Not just on the outside…

But on the inside.

Where no one could see.

Where the real battle was.

Truth

You can be free on the outside…
and still bound on the inside.

And until the inside is healed…
the cycle will try to repeat.

Scripture

2 Corinthians 10:4
"For the weapons of our warfare are not carnal, but mighty through
God to the pulling down of strong holds…"

What This Means for You

This means:

Strongholds can be pulled down.

Not managed.
Not tolerated.
Not worked around.

Destroyed.

Strongholds Don't Start Overnight

Many people think strongholds happen overnight.

But they don't.

They are built slowly.

Layer by layer.

Thought by thought.

Experience by experience.

Some strongholds are rooted in:

Trauma

Repetition

Words spoken over you

Life experiences

Pain you never processed

Things you normalized just to survive

The Deeper Layer

And some strongholds go even deeper…

They are generational.

They didn't start with you.

But they showed up in your life.

Generational Truth

There are patterns, mindsets, and struggles
that have been passed down through generations.

Cycles that move from:

Parent to child
Family to family
Generation to generation

These are often called:

Generational curses

Ancestral patterns

Inherited strongholds

And if no one confronts them…
they continue.

But Hear This Clearly

Just like negative patterns can be passed down…
so can blessings.

You are not only connected to what was broken…

You are also connected to what God has promised.

Kingdom Truth

God gives generational blessings.

That means what you break…
does not just impact you.

It impacts:

Your children

Your grandchildren

Your bloodline

Every stronghold…

stops with you.

The Decision

You are the one who says:

"It ends here"

"This will not continue through me"

"My bloodline is shifting"

Not because it's easy.

But because you are aware.

Key Insight

You are not just fighting for you…

You are breaking cycles
for generations after you.

What you confront now…

They won't have to fight later.

How to Break a Stronghold

You don't break strongholds with effort.

You don't break them with willpower.

You break them with truth.

Step 1: Identify the Lie

What have you been believing
that does not align with God's Word?

What have you accepted
as "just the way it is"?

What have you stopped questioning?

Because every stronghold
is built on a lie.

Step 2: Replace It with Truth

Find a scripture that contradicts the lie.

Stand on it.
Speak it.
Believe it.

Even when it feels unnatural.

Even when it feels uncomfortable.

Because truth will feel unfamiliar
when you've lived in a lie.

Step 3: Be Consistent

Strongholds are not built overnight
and they don't fall overnight.

But they **WILL fall**
when truth is applied consistently.

Not occasionally.

Not when you feel like it.

Consistently.

Reality Check

You cannot keep agreeing with the lie
and expect to walk in freedom.

Agreement gives it power.

Truth removes it.

Power Principle

What you feed grows.
What you starve dies.

If you keep feeding:

Fear
Pain
Old identity
Negative thinking

It will grow.

But when you starve it…

It weakens.

Activation

No more agreeing with:

Pain

Trauma

Limitation

Old identity

No more repeating what hurt you.

No more identifying with what broke you.

What You Say Now

You begin to say:

"I am free"

"I am healed"

"I am whole"

"I am new"

Even if you don't feel it yet.

Because truth is not based on feeling.

It is based on God.

Declaration

Say this out loud:

"Every stronghold in my life is being broken.

I reject every lie I have believed.
I replace it with the truth of God's Word.

Every generational cycle stops with me.
I walk in freedom, healing, and wholeness.

I am not bound.
I am not who I used to be.

I am transformed."

Prayer

Father God,

Thank You for delivering me
and continuing to heal me.

Show me every stronghold in my life
that needs to be broken.

Give me the strength to confront every lie
and replace it with Your truth.

Break every generational cycle
that has tried to follow me.

Heal every area of pain
past and present.

Let healing flow through my life
and into the generations after me.

From this day forward,
I walk in freedom,
I live in truth,
and I will not go back.

In Jesus' name,
Amen.

Chapter 5:
Authority Over The Enemy

Many believers pray…

They cry out to God.
They ask for help.
They seek answers.

But they don't walk in authority.

They ask…
They beg…
They hope…

But they don't command.

And that is where many remain stuck.

Because there is a difference between:

Having power

And walking in power

You can have access to something…
and still never use it.

Authority Has Already Been Given

God has already given you authority.

This is not something you are waiting on.

This is not something you have to earn.

This is not something you qualify for later.

It has already been released to you.

The real question is:

Do you use it?

Scripture

Luke 10:19
"Behold, I give unto you power... over all the power of the enemy..."

What This Means

Notice this:

God didn't say "some" power.

He didn't say "limited" power.

He said:

All.

That means:

You are not powerless

You are not defenseless

You are not at the mercy of the enemy

You are not waiting to be rescued

You have authority.

Truth

Authority is not something you earn.

It is something you are given.

It comes with your identity.

It comes with your position.

It comes with your relationship with God.

But if you don't know you have it…
you won't use it.

And if you don't use it…
you will live beneath what has already been provided.

Key Insight

What you don't understand,
you will not walk in.

You can sit in power…
and still live powerless
if you don't understand what belongs to you.

Why Many Believers Stay Stuck

Many believers are waiting for God
to do something…

That He has already given them power to do.

They are praying for removal…

When God said resist.

They are asking for relief…

When God gave authority.

Reality Check

Stop asking God
to remove
what He told you to resist.

Scripture Alignment

James 4:7
"Submit yourselves therefore to God. Resist the devil, and he will flee from you."

Read That Again

Notice the instruction:

You resist.

And he flees.

Not:

You ask…
You wait…
You hope…

You resist.

And resistance requires:

Awareness

Boldness

Consistency

Encouragement

There is nothing you are facing
that is uncommon to man.

What feels overwhelming to you…

Has been faced before.

What feels personal…

Is not new.

Scripture Reminder

1 Corinthians 10:13
"There hath no temptation taken you but such as is common to man…"

What This Means for You

This means:

You are not alone

You are not the only one

You are not without a way out

There is always a way through.

Always.

Truth

You have the ability to overcome
every trap
and every plan
set up by the enemy.

Not because of your strength…

But because of God's power
working through you.

Understanding Authority

Authority is not about volume.

It is about position.

You don't need to yell.
You don't need to perform.

You don't need to prove anything.

You need to know who you are.

Your Identity

You are:

A child of God

Covered by the blood

Backed by Heaven

Seated in authority

Positioned in victory

When you understand this…

Everything changes.

Power Principle

When you know who you are…

You stop tolerating
what doesn't belong to you.

You stop accepting:

Confusion

Oppression

Fear

Cycles

Delay

You stop saying:

"I guess this is just how it is"

And you start saying:

"This has to go"

Your Response

When the enemy shows up…

You don't panic.

You don't shrink.

You don't retreat.

You respond.

What You Say Matters

You say:

"No weapon formed against me shall prosper"

"I have authority over this"

"This will not take me out"

"I refuse to come into agreement with this"

"I stand in the power of God"

Because authority speaks.

Strategy Moving Forward

You must:

Speak with authority

Stand without fear

Refuse to back down

Be consistent

Not emotional intentional

Authority Is Not Passive

Authority does not sit back.

Authority does not tolerate.

Authority does not negotiate.

Authority **enforces.**

Activation

Stop shrinking.

Stop doubting.

Stop hesitating.

You don't need permission
to use what God already gave you.

You don't need validation
to walk in authority.

You already have it.

Declaration

Say this out loud:

"I walk in authority.

There is nothing I face
that I cannot overcome through God.

Every trap set for me is broken.
Every plan of the enemy is defeated.

I will not fear.

I will not shrink back.

I am covered, equipped,
and backed by Heaven.

I walk in power."

Prayer

Father God,

Thank You for giving me authority
over the enemy.

Remind me that I am not alone
and that nothing I face is beyond Your power.

Help me to walk confidently
in what You have already given me.

Strengthen me to resist the enemy
and stand firm in truth.

From this day forward,
I walk in authority,
I speak with power,
and I live in victory.

In Jesus' name,
Amen.

Chapter 6:
Standing In The Fight

Spiritual warfare is real…

And I'm not going to act like overcoming the enemy is easy.

This is not a message that ignores reality.
This is not a message that pretends everything is always simple.

Because there were times it was hard.

Times I felt tired.
Times I felt stretched.
Times I wanted to give up.

Times where continuing felt heavier than quitting.

Because we are human.

We feel.
We process.
We get tired.

But the fight we are in…

is spiritual.

And spiritual battles require a different response.

The Instruction to Stand

There comes a point in your walk with God
where the instruction is not to run…

Not to quit…

Not to step back…

But to stand.

Scripture

Ephesians 6:13
"…and having done all, to stand."

What "Standing" Really Means

Standing is not passive.

Standing is not doing nothing.

Standing is a position.

It means:

You refuse to give up

You refuse to go back

You refuse to come into agreement with defeat

You stay grounded in truth
even when everything around you feels unstable

Standing says:

"I'm still here."
"I'm still believing."
"I'm still trusting God."

Even when it's uncomfortable.

Truth

You cannot fight spiritual battles
with your flesh.

You cannot win this fight with:

Emotions

Pride

Ego

Control

Because those are all reactions.

And spiritual warfare is not won by reaction…

It is won by alignment.

What This Requires

You must trust God's Word.

Even when it's hard.
Even when it doesn't feel good.
Even when it takes time.

Even when nothing around you looks like it's changing.

Because faith is not based on what you see.

It is based on what God said.

My Reality

I mentioned in a prior chapter
that I faced divorce while married.

I've been married for over 30 years.

I met my husband at the age of 19.

We were both broken.
We were both full of sin.
We had no real role models.
No blueprint for what a healthy marriage looked like.

We were trying to build something
we had never seen.

And sometimes…

We let our egos get in the way.

What That Led To

That led to:

Arguments

Hurtful moments

Broken trust

Miscommunication

Even infidelity

And it was hard.

Not surface-level hard.

Deep hard.

The kind of hard that makes you question everything.

The kind of hard that makes you want to walk away.

Truth

Sometimes the war is not just around you…

It's in your home.
It's in your relationships.
It's in your heart.

It's in the places you don't talk about.
It's in the places you try to hold together.

And if you're not careful…

You will fight people
instead of fighting spiritually.

The Danger

You will:

Blame each other

React emotionally

Say things you don't mean

Damage what God is trying to heal

Because you're fighting in the flesh
instead of standing in the spirit.

The Turning Point

It was not until we both
trusted God with each other…

That things began to shift.

Not overnight.

Not instantly.

Not without effort.

But through a process.

The Process

A process of:

Surrender

Growth

Healing

Forgiveness

Letting go of pride

Choosing love intentionally

Learning how to respond instead of react

It wasn't easy.

But it was necessary.

Key Insight

Just because it's hard
does not mean it's not God.

Let that settle.

Because many people walk away
from what God is building…

Because it doesn't feel easy.

But God's promises still stand

Even when the process is uncomfortable.

Even when it stretches you.

Even when it requires more from you.

Scripture Alignment

Galatians 6:9
"And let us not be weary in well doing: for in due season we shall reap, if we faint not."

What This Means

Don't quit in the middle.

Don't walk away in the process.

Don't abandon what God is working on

just because it's taking time.

Because there is a **due season**.

But you only see it…

If you don't faint.

Reality Check

The enemy wants you to:

Quit too soon

Walk away too fast

Give up before breakthrough

Lose patience in the process

Abandon what God is restoring

Because if he can get you to quit…

He doesn't have to fight you anymore.

What Standing Requires

Standing requires:

Faith

Discipline

Consistency

Endurance

Emotional maturity

Spiritual alignment

It requires you to stay
when everything in you wants to leave.

Power Principle

What you keep standing on…

Will eventually produce.

Not immediately.

Not instantly.

But eventually.

Because God's Word does not return void.

Activation

Even when it's hard:

You stand.

You pray.

You trust.

You don't give up.

You don't come into agreement with defeat.

What You Say Matters

You say:

"God is working, even now"

"This will not break me"

"God's promise still stands"

"I will not quit in the process"

"I trust what God is doing even when I don't understand it"

Because your words must align

with your faith.

Declaration

Say this out loud:

"I will stand.

Even when it's hard, I will not give up.
I will not fight in my flesh.
I will trust God's Word.

Every promise God has spoken over my life
will come to pass.

I will not quit in the process.
I will stand and I will see victory."

Prayer

Father God,

Thank You for giving me the strength to stand.

Even when things are hard,
help me to trust You fully.

Teach me not to react in my flesh,
but to respond in faith.

Strengthen my heart,
steady my mind,
and anchor me in Your Word.

Help me to endure the process
and not give up before the promise.

From this day forward,
I will stand,
I will trust,

and I will not quit.

In Jesus' name,
Amen.

Chapter 7:
Walking In Victory Daily

Victory is not a moment…

It is a lifestyle.

It is not something you experience once
and then move on from.

It is something you live in daily.

You don't win one battle
and stop fighting.

You don't pray one prayer
and stop standing.

Because this walk with God
requires consistency.

Not occasional effort.
Not temporary discipline.

Daily commitment.

What Daily Victory Requires

Daily prayer.
Daily discipline.
Daily decisions.

Every day you must choose:

To believe God

To stand on His Word

To reject what is not from Him

To stay aligned

Because the enemy doesn't stop…

But neither should you.

Truth

You are not trying to become victorious.

You are already victorious.

Victory is not something you are chasing.

It is something that has already been given to you through Christ.

But here is the key:

Victory must be walked out daily.

You must live it.
You must apply it.
You must choose it every day.

Scripture

1 Samuel 30:8
"And David enquired at the Lord, saying, Shall I pursue after this troop? shall I overtake them?… Pursue: for thou shalt surely overtake them, and without fail recover all."

The Situation

David came back to Ziklag…

And everything was gone.

His family.
His possessions.

Everything he loved taken.

The place that once represented stability…
was now empty.

Burned.

Destroyed.

And in that moment…

He had a choice.

The Decision

Break…
or inquire.

React in emotion…
or respond in faith.

Give up…
or go to God.

And instead of allowing his emotions
to control him…

He went to God.

This Is Where Victory Begins

Victory does not begin
when everything looks right.

Victory begins
when you choose God
in the middle of everything going wrong.

Your Strategy: P.O.U.R.

This is how you fight.
This is how you win.
This is how you recover.

P — Pursue

You cannot sit still in warfare.

You cannot remain passive
and expect results.

You must pursue.

Pursue God.
Pursue truth.
Pursue what belongs to you.

Pursue your healing.
Pursue your purpose.
Pursue your breakthrough.

Because what you don't pursue…
you will not possess.

O — Overtake

God didn't call you just to chase…

He called you to catch.

He didn't call you to run endlessly
without results.

He called you to overtake.

That means:

You will catch up

You will regain ground

You will not be left behind

What was taken from you
will not remain lost.

U — Unfailing

God's promise does not fail.

Not sometimes.
Not eventually.

Ever.

Even when it feels delayed…
Even when it looks impossible…
Even when nothing around you makes sense…

It will not fail.

God is not inconsistent.

God is not uncertain.

God does not change His mind about what He promised.

R — Recover All

Not some.
Not partial.

All.

Everything the enemy tried to steal—

Your peace

Your joy

Your identity

Your confidence

Your purpose

Your stability

Your clarity

You will recover it.

Key Insight

Loss is not your ending.

Recovery is your portion.

What you lost
does not define you.

What you recover
will reveal who you are becoming.

Reality Check

The enemy thought he took you out…

But he only set you up
for a comeback.

What looked like loss…

Was actually positioning.

What felt like defeat…

Was preparation.

Power Principle

What you pursue with God…

You will recover with power.

Not barely.

Not weakly.

Powerfully.

Activation

This is your moment.

No more waiting.
No more hesitation.
No more fear.

You rise.

You fight.

You take it back.

What You Say Now

You say:

"I will pursue"

"I will overtake"

"I will not fail"

"I will recover all"

"I am not defeated"

"I am not behind"

"I am not disqualified"

Because victory is not coming…

Victory is already yours.

Declaration

Say this out loud:

"I walk in victory daily.

I pursue what God has for me.
I overtake every obstacle in my path.

God's promises over my life are unfailing.
Nothing He has spoken will return void.

Everything the enemy tried to steal from me
I recover it.

My peace is restored.
My joy is restored.
My life is restored.

I am victorious.
I am strong.
I am ready for war and I win."

Prayer

Father God,

Thank You for giving me victory.

Thank You that I am not defeated,
and I am not without power.

Give me the strength to pursue
everything You have called me to.

Help me to stand firm,
walk boldly,
and trust You completely.

Remind me daily
that I am victorious through You.

Everything that was lost,
everything that was broken,
everything that was stolen

I declare restoration.

From this day forward,
I walk in victory,
I fight with authority,
and I recover all.

In Jesus' name,
Amen.

Declarations

I DECLARE WAR — ACCORDING TO THE WORD

I declare:

I am not defeated.
I am more than a conqueror through Him that loves me.
(Romans 8:37)

I am not powerless.
God has not given me the spirit of fear,
but of power, love, and a sound mind.
(2 Timothy 1:7)

I declare:

My mind is guarded.
I cast down every imagination
and every high thing that exalts itself
against the knowledge of God.
(2 Corinthians 10:5)

I think on things that are true, honest, just, pure, and of good report.
(Philippians 4:8)

I declare:

The Word of God is my weapon.
It is alive, powerful, and sharper than any two-edged sword.
(Hebrews 4:12)

I will speak the Word boldly.
"It is written" will be my response in every battle.
(Matthew 4:4)

I declare:

Every stronghold in my life is broken.

The weapons of my warfare are not carnal,
but mighty through God
to the pulling down of strongholds.
(2 Corinthians 10:4)

Whom the Son sets free is free indeed.
(John 8:36)

I declare:

I walk in authority.
God has given me power over all the power of the enemy.
(Luke 10:19)

I submit to God,
I resist the devil,
and he must flee.
(James 4:7)

No weapon formed against me shall prosper.
(Isaiah 54:17)

I declare:

I will stand.
Having done all, I stand firm.
(Ephesians 6:13)

I will not grow weary in well doing,
for in due season I shall reap if I do not faint.
(Galatians 6:9)

I declare:

I walk in victory daily.
I pursue, I overtake, and I recover all.
(1 Samuel 30:8)

Thanks be to God,
who gives me the victory

through Jesus Christ.
(1 Corinthians 15:57)

I declare:

I am strong in the Lord
and in the power of His might.
(Ephesians 6:10)

I am covered.
I am equipped.
I am backed by Heaven.

FINAL DECLARATION

I do not speak my feelings
I speak the Word.

I do not move by what I see
I move by what God said.

This is not just confession…
This is alignment with Heaven.

I DECLARE WAR—AND I WALK IN VICTORY

Final Charge

This is not just a book.

This is a call to war.

You now know:

- The battlefield
- The strategy
- The weapons
- Your authority

So now

Stand. Speak. Fight. Win.

About the Author

Sherrell Attaway is a dynamic woman of faith, a marketplace leader, and a transformational voice committed to helping people turn their purpose into progress.

With a heart rooted in service, she has built her life and career around one core mission:

Helping people transform their lives spiritually, financially, and practically.

She is a verified life coach, tax professional, and business owner who leads a successful tax company with a growing team. Alongside her husband, she is actively involved in real estate investing, specializing in fix-and-flip properties and wealth-building strategies.

In addition, she serves as a licensed mortgage loan officer, equipping individuals and families with the knowledge and access needed to become homeowners and build generational wealth.

But her impact does not stop in business.

Sherrell Attaway is a pastor and international ministry leader who carries a powerful message of faith, discipline, and transformation. As a sought-after speaker, she travels to encourage, equip, and empower individuals to overcome limitations and walk boldly in their God-given purpose.

She is also a mentor and teacher, committed to developing others through guidance, wisdom, and real-life application. Her passion for service extends through her nonprofit organization, **Ignite (It Only Takes a Spark)**, where she focuses on inspiring change and creating opportunities for growth in others.

As a Christian faith-based author, Pastor Attaway writes with both spiritual depth and practical strategy—bridging the gap between faith and execution. She is the author of *God, Battle Your War* and

Bending in the Battlefield, powerful works that equip readers to understand spiritual warfare, strengthen their faith, and stand firm in life's battles.

Through her writing and teaching, she emphasizes the power of **marketplace ministry**, showing that purpose is not limited to the pulpit but can be lived out in business, leadership, and everyday life.

She is also the visionary behind a faith-based apparel brand, using fashion as a form of expression, encouragement, and ministry.

Her life and message are built on a simple but powerful principle:

First Pray. Then Plan. Then Execute.

Through every role she carries, Pastor Attaway remains committed to one assignment:

To help others recognize what's already inside of them…

and give them the tools, faith, and strategy to turn their passion into a paycheck.

"Empowering purpose. Building discipline. Producing results.

NOW
BOOKING
2026
PASTOR SHERRELL ATTAWAY
PASTOR • PROPHETESS • REVIVALIST
BOOKING INFO:
PHONE: (404) 410-6455
EMAIL: PastorAttaway@gmail.com